101 ESSENTIAL LISTS
FOR PRIMARY TEACHERS

101 ESSENTIAL LISTS SERIES

101 ESSENTIAL LISTS
FOR PRIMARY
TEACHERS

Fred Sedgwick

continuum
LONDON • NEW YORK

Continuum International Publishing Group
The Tower Building   80 Maiden Lane
11 York Road   Suite 704
London   New York
SE1 7NX   NY 10038

www.continuumbooks.com

First published in 2006

British Library Cataloguing-in-Publication Data
A catalogue record for this book is available from the British Library.

ISBN: 0-8264-8871-4 (paperback)

Library of Congress Cataloging-in-Publication Data
A catalog record for this book is available from the Library of Congress.

Typeset by YHT Ltd
Printed and bound in Great Britain by Ashford Colour Press Ltd,
Gosport, Hampshire

CONTENTS

ACKNOWLEDGEMENTS

People who have helped me with this book, and to whom I am grateful:

Duncan Bathgate, Helen Butcher, Joan Deakin, Matthew Garbutt, Dorothy Hampson, Mary Moore, Linda Parkinson, John Parkinson, Laurie Rousham, Anita Sedgwick, Cate Stafford and, especially, Christina Garbutt, my editor, who took great care over my book.

For my son Daniel, as always

TWO NOTES

1

Many a fine poem is made up of a list. Many a fine prayer is, too. And for some of us, the list of tasks that confront us, scribbled in the kitchen in the morning, is a comfort. And it grows more comforting as, during the day, we move down the list, ticking off the tasks as we have done them. Readers will make their own lists; here's some I prepared earlier.

2

When I write about curriculum subjects (Lists 48–58), I write about them mainly in terms of their aesthetic content. This is because the aesthetics in many subjects (PE and Mathematics, to take two examples) are largely ignored. By 'aesthetic', I mean to do with the senses, and, by extension, to do with perception of beauty.

A Fulfilled Human Being 1

LIST 1   A rounded human being

You can't be a fulfilled teacher without being a fulfilled human being. Self-respect

- ○ in the home (pre-eminently there, obviously)
- ○ in the street
- ○ in the pub
- ○ in the restaurant
- ○ in the gym
- ○ in places of worship
- ○ on the football terraces

is a prerequisite for self-respect in the classroom. The teacher lives in the same wide, exhilarating, disturbing world ('crazier and more of it than we think' as Louis MacNeice puts it, in his poem 'Snow') as everyone else.

And the most basic part of that world is – what do we eat?

LIST 2 Food

Some of what follows is a counsel of perfection, and should be followed only as general rules. Indeed, I suspect that a day without a bun, a Twix bar, a pork pie, a toasted teacake, a bacon sandwich with white bread, so that the bacon fat seeps through the snowy, sugary whiteness – not the healthy brown I'd customarily use – is a day wasted. Nevertheless ...

- Make good food a central part of your life. As Dr Johnson said, 'a man who doesn't care about what he puts into himself will care about nothing'.
- Never miss breakfast.
- Fruit and vegetables
  The 'five-a-day' movement has become a cliché in schools, but, like most clichés, it holds a lot of truth. Stock up on three of the five by drinking fresh orange juice, eating an apple or a banana, and dropping grapes on cereal at breakfast.
- See food as more than stocking up on fuel. Learn about it. The Saturday and Sunday newspapers (the *Guardian* and the *Observer*, the two *Telegraph*s, the two *Independent*s, *The Times* and the *Sunday Times*) provide what amounts to an informal Open University course on this.
- Distinguish between processed and fresh, between fish coming from vanishing stocks and fish still plentiful, between chickens that have happy-ish lives, and those that have spent their lives in cages, between vegetables that are in season, and vegetables that aren't.

More about food

○ Notwithstanding what I wrote earlier, avoid bread, especially processed white bread. It gives a rush of energy with its sugar ... then that rush fades, and lets you down mid-afternoon.

○ Eat salad as often as possible, at least between April and September, when the weather suits a salad, and a salad suits the weather.

○ Eat seasonal vegetables. Learn to like root vegetables, swedes, turnips and parsnips in the autumn and winter, and sprouts in the winter. And asparagus in its season. Implicit in this is: avoid, as far as possible, foods that have travelled hundreds of air miles, like asparagus from Peru.

○ If you live in the country, find a farm shop or a farmers' market, and use it.

○ Eat pasta and rice as staples, not just potatoes.

○ Eat out, if you can afford it, at least once a week, with your partner or with friends. Take your time. Relish the tastes and the company. If you're on your own, take a book.

○ Buy the best ingredients you can afford.

LIST 4 **Drink**

○ Drink water. The modern habit of sipping it all day, however drearily trendy, is a good one. Watch out, though: a friend of mine, a comprehensive headteacher, habitually sipped water during morning assembly. The teachers were fond of him – he almost defined the words 'jovial' and 'kind' – and one day, at 9 am, they secretly substituted neat gin for water.

○ Never drink beer or wine, or anything else with alcohol, at lunchtime. Strange to say, thirty years ago, teachers often went to the pub on Fridays at lunchtime, and drank. How we didn't sleep through the afternoon, I don't know.

○ When drinking wine with a meal, or at a party, alternate each glass with a glass of water.

○ Keep personal rules: never drink till 6 o'clock in the evening, for example.

○ Finally, 'a man who exposes himself when he is intoxicated, has not the art of getting drunk' (Samuel Johnson).

LIST 5 Ways of getting exercise without going to a gym

○ Walk two miles every day. One reason that some Americans are obese (the cheeks of their arses in different states, as Bill Bryson puts it) is that their cities are not designed for walking. Ours are.

○ Leave the car at home, and collect the Sunday papers on foot. When shopping, park a mile away from the stores, and thereby get two miles in painlessly.

○ To help meet this target, wear a pedometer, and aim to get to 8,000 paces (about two miles) every day.

○ Park at the top of multi-storey car parks. Run up to the car when you've finished shopping. Shove slower climbers aside. Yes, I know about the bags. Get your partner to carry those. I've found that car park attendants worry, as they watch you on CCTV driving to the empty ninth level. Are you are going to throw yourself off the top because of some ghastly personal loss? Disabuse them.

○ Learn to love the local park, or, if you're lucky, the seashore, or the estuaries, or the hills, or the lakes, or mountains, and use them often. Find out the names of flora and fauna. Study them.

○ Take the dog out.

○ Ride a bicycle.

○ Play a sport: five-a-side football, indoor cricket, tennis.

○ If you can (I wish I could), swim.

○ If you've had no exercise during the day, trot around the garden, sometimes running on the spot. You'll feel a fool, but you won't be one.

Spiritual well-being: the arts

You are not a machine. There is something inside you that resists the market. You sense it when you watch waves breaking on a foreign shore, or when you make love, or when you pray. There are many ways of finding that something. One is through the arts.

○ Read. Many teachers say they have no time to read. But steeping yourself in another world through a novel or a biography, or an autobiography, helps you to concentrate on other people's problems, and puts yours in perspective. Reading gives practice in dealing with your own problems.
○ Find one writer you like, and read her every word.
○ Listen to music, not just as a background. Make it, like food, a central part of your life.
○ Become an authority on one kind of music. Mozart? Hip-hop? Country and Western? Bebop jazz?
○ Find one composer or performer you like, and hear his every note.
○ Find an artist you like, and see every painting she's painted, or every sculpture she's sculpted. In reproduction, probably, but ...
○ Go to galleries often.

It is exhausting to look at art for any length of time. This is because encountering art is an intense emotional and intellectual experience.

Spiritual well-being: religion

○ If you are a believer, pray.
○ Find a place of worship that you feel both comfortable with and challenged by, and go there. I find this difficult. Too many clergymen are too keen to handshake you out of church after the service; and have no interest in you, really. Keep trying.
○ If you aren't a believer, meditate.
○ If you're not sure, say what the centurion said, when his servant, he thought (wrongly) was dying: 'Lord I believe, help thou mine unbelief.'
○ If you are committed to one religion, find out about others.

Spiritual well-being: personally

○ Retain and develop at least one interest that began at university or college.

○ Retain, or get, one interest that is utterly unlike your professional work: watching the local football team (or, better, playing for it), hang-gliding or flower-arranging, learning Spanish.

○ Use holidays not only as physical, but also as spiritual, recreation. Become an expert on one place: a Greek island, the Mumbles peninsula in Wales, a range of hills in the north of England, a foreign city.

○ Keep a journal on holidays and give it, as a Christmas present, to your partner.

○ Keep a professional journal emphasizing your triumphs, however minor, in the classroom.

○ Concentrate on someone else's needs for a period every day. This is called 'love'.

○ Keep in touch with friends; if possible, from all stages of your life: school, college, first job, second job, those people you met in a swimming pool on Lanzarote or Ibiza. Who knows when you will need them, and they you?

○ Involve yourself in something outside education.

○ Don't beat yourself up about things: many government ideas will disappear soon, and there are many you shouldn't worry about. Who remembers the Russian poet Pushkin's censors? But millions remember his poems.

○ Every day, do one job that you have been putting off.

A Fulfilled Teacher   2

That was all about being a fulfilled human being. But eventually you have to consider yourself as a special kind of human being, a teacher.

 Reasons for low morale

Morale among teachers is often low. Listing some of the causes is all too easy:

- Ofsted's on its way, or is here, or will be coming soon, or eventually, like death.
- Administrative tasks take over valuable hours. There are forms to be pored over, and weekends are lost. Instead of being filled with walks in the park, or visits to the seaside with the children, they are spent on meaningless tasks. A poet spending time on a tax return could not be more frustrated than a teacher writing short-, medium- and long-term plans on a Sunday afternoon.
- In some schools, children or parents present problems.
- Some teachers get little help in schools.
- Some teachers feel that they work with colleagues who don't believe in the benefits of teaching at all, or in the children.

But there are ...

Reasons for rejoicing in your choice of profession

○ You work with human beings – children – who are, by and large, happy and honest.

○ You have great power. You may be frightened of inspectors, but, as Andrew Davies's character Prin says, in his play of that name, 'Eventually they have to go away. They have to go away and leave you with the children. And then it begins.'

○ When they are taught properly, children sing in assembly well enough to lift the saddest teacher's heart.

○ Their noise on the playground speaks about their relative innocence and about their unconscious delight in their common humanity.

○ You transform them every day. Or rather, you enable them to transform themselves; not only intellectually, but morally, spiritually and socially.

An inspector told my friend that, at the age of ten, he was rebellious and unhappy; that his family was dysfunctional; and that he was transformed by a teacher who sat him down and said: 'Now what you need is a good listening to.'

○ In fact, you transform yourself, because by teaching you learn. And by learning, you learn to teach better. The whole process is a virtuous, as opposed to a vicious, circle.

○ You can often see the learning happening. There are moments when you see ignorance change into knowledge (their knowledge, mostly, but sometimes yours). A sudden smile confirms new understanding, or a displacement of bafflement.

More reasons for rejoicing

○ Children say things that lift the heart. One ten-year-old girl had as much passion for poetry as I have. She merely had less knowledge and experience of it. When, tired and smelling of chalk dust and felt tips, I walked to the car park to begin the long drive home from her north London school, she ran up to me and said, 'Will I ever see you again?'

○ Things you say today will be remembered in thirty years' time. Watch out, though. It's worth making a list of things your teachers said to you, and then dividing it into two: one positive and one negative. I find the negative memories from my schooldays outweigh the positive ...

○ Your colleagues are people of integrity. If I had to lose my wallet, or my mobile phone, or my dignity anywhere, I'd choose a staffroom. You are unlikely to come across diseases like racism, or sexism. They may be there, though, dangerously suppressed.

○ You are in the same job as Socrates, the Buddha and Jesus.

Teacher morale is, to some extent, a matter of presentation.

What do children notice in the morning about you?

Things to be aware of in your appearance in the morning

Much as you can learn about what a school is like by simply walking into the entrance, children can learn about their teacher's mood with their first glimpse in the morning.

- Facial expression – smile or frown? Is it welcoming?
- Badges: wear an interesting one, one that says something about you. They provide talking points, especially with young children. I sometimes wear a Fungus the Bogeyman badge myself. Badges denoting football affiliations interest boys.
- Jewellery. One child fingered a Greek onyx ring I used to wear, and said 'That's lovely'. Children are alert to details.
- Bright colours.
- Interesting ties.
- Clothes, above all, that you are comfortable wearing.
- Clothes that are practical for the messy, painty, dirty situation where your calling has placed you.

That word 'calling' reminds me of a teacher in George Harpole's school (see List 95) who sang only one line in John Keble's hymn 'Forth in thy name'. It was 'Preserve me from my calling's snare.'

LIST 13 — The kind of clothes you shouldn't wear

The cavalier in me denounces:

- ○ grey clothes
- ○ navy ones
- ○ dowdy ones
- ○ what you wore yesterday.

I met a teacher who wore the same uniform every day. The colours were various shades of dark brown. She stuffed it in the washing machine on Friday, and put it on again on Monday. What does this tell us (or, more importantly, what did it tell her class) about a) her attitude to the job and b) her morale?

- ○ dark suits with dark ties (men) and floppy bows (women).

The puritan in me denounces:

- ○ Low-cut tops and trousers that expose your underwear, tattoos and, builder-wise, the top of the cleft between your buttocks
- ○ and for men, T-shirts and shorts.

It is odd that headteachers in schools that have the strictest uniform codes often allow men on the staff to dress as if they're at the Kop end of their football ground on a warm autumn Saturday.

How they see us

Here is an insight from a student in a residential secondary school.

○ Resident tutors
  Glum, with grey-purple under their eyes after a night of too much Red Bull, and a lack of sleep from loud teenagers.

○ Art teachers
  After 10 am they all need another coffee (brought in on a paint palette and put back on the permanent coffee rings on the desk). They're all dreary until they get into the art room.

○ History teachers
  Grouchy and irritable every morning. Smartly dressed with large frowns, they never fail to storm down the corridors and silence the 1st years.

○ English teachers
  Same as they always are; not quite ready for anything, always willing to watch a film that is distantly related to the subject. Some are brooding, wearing the trademark leather jacket.

○ Music teachers
  They walk in readily, but can't stand loud noise until break time. Every morning eccentric and ready to go, always encouraging the upcoming musicians.

○ Sport teachers
  Never yet arrived without a tanned face from a skiing holiday, they have probably already been for a jog around the cross-country course twice, and by 9 o'clock think that everyone is as awake as them. They always seem at their brightest in the mornings as they walk down sunny paths in their track suits, with whistles round their necks.

Writing an application letter

This is your first presentation of yourself to a potential headteacher and a governing body. What might it convey of your personality?

Your prose style is one thing. Evidence of care taken is another. And any hint of a life away from the classroom that you give is yet another.

○ Today it is almost universal to word-process application letters.
○ If you hand-write, do it with style, clarity and a fountain pen. And do it on decent A4 paper, not on a notepad.
○ Don't be pretentious. One candidate wrote to me, when I was a headteacher seeking a deputy, that she was interested in (I am not making this up) 'in ascending order of importance: Astro-physics; Beekeeping; Philosophy; Children'.
○ Follow the old-fashioned rules of letter-writing: your address top right, the receiving address next left, 'yours sincerely' if you've addressed the head by name, 'yours faithfully' if you haven't.
○ Do at least one draft. Probably two. Possibly three. It's much easier if you word-process, of course.
○ Get a friend to read over the draft, and to be critical. He or she is your crap-detector.
○ Keep sentences mostly short, or medium in length.
○ Always photocopy your completed form, so that when you apply for another post, the task is largely (though not completely – you will have changed your mind over some things!) clerical.

George Orwell's rules for clear prose; adapted by me

These apply here. Clarity is everything, and Orwell is brilliant on clarity. Here are his rules:

○ Don't use clichés – any figure of speech that has been used countless times before. For a list of educational clichés to be avoided, see List 93.

Even if your clichés aren't recognized as such by the reader, and they probably won't be, they have a deadening effect overall.

○ Use the short word, not the long one. 'Tries', for example, not 'attempts'. 'Uses', not 'utilizes'. (What is that word *for*?)

There is in many writers a half-submerged belief that long words are evidence of intelligence. They aren't.

○ Where one word will do, don't use two. 'Before' rather than 'prior to' or 'ahead of'.
○ Check whether any of your words are redundant. 'Very' almost always is, for example. It is here: 'I am very enthusiastic about games teaching.' Most adjectives and adverbs are redundant; they are fat: verbs and nouns are the muscles and bones of language. A sentence should be lithe, not obese. So,
  – If you can cut a word out, do.
  – Use the active mode rather than the passive. Not 'the work was enjoyed by the class' but 'the class enjoyed the work'.

Preparing for an interview

- ○ Get fit. Eat good food, take early nights, drink less booze than usual.
- ○ Read *The Times Educational Supplement* carefully for the two weeks before your interview. And the *Education Guardian*, published with the main paper on Tuesdays. Make notes about the issues of the day.
- ○ Ask if you can visit the school. If they say no, wonder why.
- ○ Research the school. Chew the fat, get the gossip, dish the dirt. Find out as much as possible, while recognizing that not all you hear will be reliable.
- ○ Talk about your work with anyone who will listen.
- ○ Get a colleague, or, better still, a panel of colleagues, to put you through a dummy interview. I've done this, on both sides of the table. Your colleagues will take the mick, and work hard to put you ill at ease. They will be harder on you than a real panel. It is good preparation.
- ○ Read your copy of your letter and form immediately before leaving for the interview.

LIST 18 Things to remember in the interview

○ Take a deep breath before every answer. This not only helps you speak better, it also gives you time for thought.

○ Make eye contact with your questioner, but don't intimidate them.

○ Remember: someone on the panel is more nervous than you are. I've been on both sides, many times, and I know. If you can see who it is, work on putting that person at ease.

○ If you are asked a question like 'Do you think there is still a place in schools for Drama/Art/Dance?' or whatever, do not begin: 'I hope so'. This invites the irritated response, 'I am not asking you what you hope, but what you think.'

○ The chair of the panel will ask you whether you will accept the post if you are offered it. Be prepared to answer then. It is very bad form to turn down a job after you've been offered it.

Questions they may ask you

Have answers prepared for these questions:

- What do you think of the latest legislation? (Whatever it might be: hence your study of the education pages.)
- What is your weakest subject?
- What will you do to become stronger in it?
- How do you deal with disruption?
- Have you had experience with children with dyslexia/autism/ Asperger's syndrome? Tell us about it.
- What will you bring to this school that's unique to you?
- Your present school is in a very different area from this one. Do you think that will present problems for you? Or for us?
- Describe a successful lesson from your own experience.
- Who is the greatest influence on your work as a teacher?
- What steps would you take to make sure there was no discrimination in your classroom?
- What hobbies do you have? Could you use them in the classroom?

Playing the piano is a significant ability in schools, though you may worry about being labelled as the assembly accompanist. Many a private enthusiasm – folk dancing, learning Spanish, playing blues guitar – could enliven an after-school club. Or a lesson, come to that.

- Sum up briefly your answer to the question, What is education for?
- Or, Define the purpose of teaching.

For one answer, see the last words in this book. Another is from the educationist Lawrence Stenhouse: 'the purpose of education is to make us freer and more creative' (*An Introduction to Curriculum Design and Development*).

Questions you should ask

○ Always have some questions in mind for the moment near the end when the person chairing the interview says 'And is there anything you would like to ask us?'

For example:

○ Do you encourage educational visits in this school?
○ and school journeys?
○ What is the school's policy about ...? Some examples might be: inclusion, anti-discrimination, school journeys, animals in the school, sex education, parent–teacher associations, governor involvement in the curriculum ...
○ What are the school meals like?
○ Is healthy eating encouraged in both the canteen and the classroom?
○ How does the Parent Teacher Association work?
○ Do governors get involved in the classrooms?

Preparing for Ofsted

In the weeks before the inspection

○ Remember that your classroom is an interesting place and be more aware than usual of what is happening in it. In quiet moments, study it like a sociologist, or a journalist, as if you're going to write a chapter or an article about it, or like an artist, as if you're going to draw it.

○ Ask your Teaching Assistant (TA) to watch carefully as well, and discuss your teaching with her. Many a thoughtful parent who has become a friend can perform this role.

○ Consider your strengths: your methods of control, the way you can reproach a child silently with a raised eyebrow, encourage a child with a smile or a wink, and how you know which gestures are right for which child, how you can, as a teacher said to Edward Blishen, 'pin them to their desks with the right sort of glare'.

○ Remember your skills in your best subjects. Reflect on past successes.

○ Consider your weaknesses, too, but not with much deliberation: this is, after all, a time for positive thinking.

○ Remember you are almost certainly more vigorous mentally than the inspector, if not as well weighed down with a little brief authority.

○ Prepare the children. One book suggests, cynically, that you get the children to raise their right hand if they know an answer, their left if they don't.

LIST 22 Ways of understanding what a school is

Tick the definition(s) that you agree with.

A school is:

(a) a means of producing tomorrow's workers, for offices, factories and farms
(b) a means of inculcating children with society's values and cultural heritage
(c) a means of enabling children to criticize society's values and cultural heritage
(d) a means of setting children free to understand themselves, their world, and their relationship to that world.

If you ticked (a) you should be working in a school in a Dickens novel. Is your name Gradgrind, by any chance? (see *Hard Times*, by Charles Dickens: the first few pages will do). If you ticked (b) you should phone the Duchy of Cornwall, and get an advisory job with the Prince of Wales. If you ticked (c) you are a dangerous radical, and the *Daily Mail* will be after you. If you ticked (d) you are a soggy liberal. Put that *Guardian* down right now!

Even if you do not consider yourself a political animal, it is well to be aware of your ideological position.

And what a schoolchild is

○ an empty vessel, waiting to be filled with knowledge

or

○ a partly full vessel, with the contents awaiting transformation

○ a passive individual to whom things are done

or

○ an active one who is capable of doing things

○ a child comes to you with 'Nil on entry'

or

○ a child comes to you full of information about the world, some wrong, some right, all of it partial

In other words, education is

○ a matter of yelling all the facts the child needs down a speaking tube (transmission model)

or

○ an apparatus which will help the child to interpret the world for herself (interpretative model)

In the classroom

Teaching is about what happens when you are alone with the children.

o the bosses
o the managerialists
o the politicians
o the inspectors
o the suited ones
o what Prin disgracefully calls 'little jacks-in-office'
o maybe even the governors
o sections of the press

will tell you, or at least imply, something else. But teaching is not about test results and league tables; it is not about statistics at all (see my List 91, Damned lies, for more on this). It is about what happens in the classroom, when you talk to the children, and they talk to you, and (even more important, sometimes) when they talk to each other.

Where does learning happen?

Many schools, backed by the government, throw up their hands in moralizing bafflement when parents take children out of school during term time. 'How can we deliver the National Curriculum', they ask, 'when a child is away for two weeks in July?' I took my son out of school once for the first two weeks of the autumn term. We went to Malta, and saw prehistoric sites, art galleries and churches. We ate pizzas in Republic Square, watched football at the National Stadium, and walked miles around Valletta and in the surrounding countryside. The ruling political party sent deafening flares into the sky as we lay on beaches. We made friends with other English people. And the National Curriculum has more to offer than that …?

The best learning happens:

○ out in the world
○ under the sun and the clouds
○ in fields
○ by rivers
○ in streets
○ at home
○ in art galleries
○ in churches, synagogues, mosques and temples
○ in museums.

But nearly all teaching is restricted to classrooms. We should learn Monet's lesson, revolutionary in the life of art, that we learn most out of doors. And if not out of doors, out of classrooms.

But, damn it, we have to concentrate on the classroom.

How much time is wasted in schools! Minutes evaporate as children wait listlessly for something meaningless to be done. It has been the custom to do things – things that have a long history – that don't need to be done, or at least don't need to be done in the way that they are customarily done.

Some time-wasting activities

○ Children sit in silence while the register is called.

'Good morning Norman. Bonsoir Marguerite.' Doesn't it make you want to puke? People tell me that this is necessary for security's sake, but TAs could easily do the registers, looking round the room as the children begin work. And the 'Good mornings', in whatever language, don't make it any better.

○ The first class arrives in assembly fifteen minutes before the last.

That first class is then subjected to what I might call, with exaggeration, torture. But you try it. Sit silently on a floor with your legs crossed for a quarter of an hour, and see how you feel.

○ In lessons, children must wait for basic equipment as the teacher gives it out.

What is going on during this time? Much of whatever the teacher has said in her attempt to inspire the children has leaked away. It is merely a chance for the children to natter about non-school issues, or to resume, or to begin, fights.

More time-wasting activities

○ The word queue

In some schools, children have to wait for their words before they can continue their writing. In the queue, the third child is always the same child. That child doesn't want to get to the front. She is enjoying time out, and repeatedly offers her place to the child behind. And the child at the end is about to be disappointed to find that the teacher doesn't know how to spell 'pterodactyl' or 'accommodation' either.

○ Before beginning, children must write the date, the title, the learning objective and must rule a margin. Meanwhile, whatever inspiration you breathed into them leaks away.

○ Lining up at the end of breaks.

The whistle blasts. They stand still. It blasts again. They move into lines. It blasts again. They file into their classrooms. 'Why?' as Harold Rosen once asked. 'It's not the bloody army.'

○ Children reading scheme books aloud to adults. How much adult reading is reading aloud? This is not teaching and learning, it is a crude form of assessment.

Non-educational matters that affect children's learning

○ Have they eaten breakfast? In some schools, it is worth starting a breakfast club. This is bread cast upon the waters, and thou shalt find it after many days: money spent will be repaid in the children's learning. Fruit, milk and cereal are the basics.

○ What are school dinners like? Jamie Oliver has done children a favour by highlighting the mean funds and lousy quality of school meals. But it is possible that his television programmes were seeds that fell on stony ground 'and sprung up ... and because they had no root, they withered away'. In any case, most things in my first list apply here.

○ And the internal environment? Gloomy, dark classrooms, poorly cleaned, affect everyone's morale, especially the children's.

○ And what about the area outside the classrooms? You can't supply grass where, as in many inner-city schools, there is none; but you can brighten the playground with hopscotch courts, big plastic games of chess and Connect 4, climbing frames, scooters and small bikes.

○ And what about the children's homes, and the streets, and the park where they play? Edward Blishen noted in his diary that 'the primary need is not education, but decent surroundings'. You can't do anything about these, but you can be aware of them, and take them into consideration when children behave badly – or when they behave well.

LIST 30   Some activities for children during these waiting moments

○ Put poetry books around the room, and ask the children to find three poems they like, and to read them to each other.

○ The same with art books. The children should choose pictures, and discuss with each other why they like them. Art books can be had for very little money in remainder shops. You could equip a library with excellent reproductions for less than £300.

○ Write a short poem on the board, and ask the children to learn it by heart.

○ Put up an OHP of previously learned words, such as the months or the days. But put it on upside down, and tell the children they have to copy the words down the right way up. Then turn the OHP around.

○ Put a picture or a cartoon up, and ask the children to think of a caption for it. It should be as long as possible.

○ Put a series of three words on the board. Ask the children to identify the odd one out. There may be more than one right answer. Allow any that they can justify. Your odd ones out should be for other reasons than meaning: pronunciation, grammatical function, one is palindromic and the others aren't.

Questions that teachers ask children: to be avoided

○ Questions that they don't need the answer to, so why ask them?

Examples

Why are you doing that?
This uses up your time and, more importantly, your emotional energy as the child answers (or maybe does not) truthfully (or untruthfully). And you almost certainly know why he's doing that! Why bother? Live longer. Don't wind yourself up, or allow children to. It's better to say, 'Please stop doing that.'

Would you do that at home?
As Michael Rosen has pointed out in a poem, this is always followed by 'Then why do it here?' if the answer is 'No', and 'Well, don't do it here' if the answer is 'Yes'.

○ Questions that are not really questions, but orders.

Examples

Would you like to come and sit on the carpet?
Would you like to come down from the climbing frame now?
Would you like to put that away now?

It is important to understand that four- and five-year-olds do not hear these as orders, but as real questions. So when they say 'No', they are not being subversive.

○ Questions that are attempts to find out how much information has stuck. In asking these closed questions, we are concerned with a crude form of assessment.

Examples

What was the name of the Viking ships?
Who was Henry VIII's first wife?

Assessment may be an important part of a teacher's life, but it is not as important as teaching. And this assessment is hit-and-miss.

LIST 32 Questions to be thought about and asked

These may lead to learning. Anything can be taught by asking this sort of question. This is Socrates' way. Some examples:

In history

○ Can you tell me why the Viking longships were the shape they were?
○ How do you think Henry VIII felt when his new queen's baby was a girl?

In science

○ Can you see any birds on the field? What are they doing? Why are they doing it?

In language

○ Can you see any ways that this poet uses alliteration to make his poem better? And what is that alliteration for?

In geography

○ Can you find a place on this map that shows mountains/ rivers ...?

In PE

○ What would be the best way to move from balancing in one way, and balancing in another?

Generally

○ Do you think ...

Almost any question beginning like this is a genuine question, especially if it is followed up with 'Why do you think that?' and plenty of time (however uncomfortable it feels) in which the child is allowed to think.

Making friends with a new class

o What's your name?

This involves you telling the children your first name, and stories behind it. For example, who gave you your name? What does it mean? Are you named after anyone in the family, or out of it? Do you like your name? If you do, why do you? If not, why not?

You then invite the children to tell similar stories about their names, and eventually to research at home with relatives the answers to these and other questions. A useful help here is a dictionary of names.

But there are no dictionaries that I know of that list names from the Islamic, Hindu and Sikh traditions. Make a virtue of necessity. If you have many children from these traditions in your class, compile one. Make it school-wide. County-wide. It might be publishable.

This project energizes the tired old Myself project!

Another friend-making activity

The box

This involves thinking, or praying, or meditating and then writing in answer to these questions:

○ There's a box in your head, made of three beautiful things. What are they?
○ It opens in a way that's like you. Are you loud? Are you thoughtful? Are you a dancer/a rider/Are you religious ... How does it open?
○ There's a secret in the box. What is it?
○ There are three precious memories in your box. What are they?

It helps if you have prepared some answers to these questions. For example: 'My box is made of jazz, the smell of mimosa in Spain, and my son's voice saying "Hello Dad" when I haven't seen him for a long time ... It opens slowly, as slowly as a tortoise's head peeping out after hibernation ... In my box is my love of Louis Armstrong's trumpet ... I remember when I held my son for the first time, and my mother's last smile, and a cloud that floated in the sky when I held hands with my first girlfriend ... '

Organizing the classroom: Introduction

What is an efficient room like? As so often, learning, like other parts of children's lives, should be like learning and other parts of adults' lives. A child-writer, for example, should have the same opportunities and practices (and should expect the same problems) as a professional writer. By the same token, an efficient room for children should be like an efficient room for adults.

So think of your kitchen, or your living room.

You need:

○ easy movement around the room.
○ a décor that is suitable for the activity practised there.
○ Each room should contain the equipment for cooking, or reading, or listening to music, or watching television, and this equipment should be conveniently placed or stored.
○ And it should be the best that you can afford.

All of this goes for classrooms.

LIST 36 Equipment and arrangement

○ Children should have the necessary equipment to hand (paper and pencils or pens for writing, for example).

Otherwise there is a gap between lighting-up time – when you inspire them – and work, when they should be writing or drawing, or experimenting or researching. In this gap, if someone comes round giving out paper etc., inspiration will leak away. The teacher isn't a guardian of equipment. She doesn't have to give it out. It isn't *hers*. It should be readily available for the children. It is *theirs*. And a child shouldn't waste his time, and everyone else's, giving it out either. What a dull word 'monitor' is!

○ There should always be a choice of materials: pens, pencils, different papers for writing, for example. All immediately to hand.

As the educationist Robin Tanner wrote, 'all choice in a classroom involves a measure of learning'.

○ The equipment should be the best that is affordable.
○ It should be easy to walk around the room, without contorting the body so that it edges uncomfortably round desks and cupboards.

When desks are arranged in rows, so that the children can better concentrate on that altar, the teacher's desk, there is less floor space. Children should be arranged in groups, facing each other. This is, firstly, because they can plan tasks together. Secondly, it offers more space. When they need to face the altar, they can turn their chairs round.

Organizing the quality of the classroom

○ Books should be invitingly displayed; picture books at Key Stage 1 with their front covers, not their spines showing.

○ Tatty books should be rooted out and binned every term.

○ If you have a computer suite, it takes the machines out of everyday life. It makes them special. We *visit* a computer suite. On the contrary, a computer should be an everyday tool, available in the classroom when it is needed. Not to be visited.

○ Star charts showing who's learned their tables, or who can spell 'February', or who's got the most 'Headteacher's stars' make some children depressed, some conceited, and most indifferent. Do you want depression, conceit and indifference in your classroom? These charts face all of them with information (worthless though it is) that should be confidential.

○ Alphabets are ignored after the first day, especially when displayed 10 feet high.

○ So are posters of tables.

Redundant things

Examine your classroom. Is there anything in it that isn't useful?

There is no need for:

- 30 dictionaries
- 30 thesauruses
- 30 atlases
- 30 Bibles

Are they all going to need them all at the same time? Get two of each of these valuable books, and spend the saved money on fiction, poetry, art books, books celebrating science, technology, history, geography and art.

- broken equipment

What is that old computer doing there, with its pathetic post-it saying 'I don't work'?

- out of date equipment, especially globes and maps with countries – Czechoslovakia, the USSR, Yugoslavia – that no longer exist.
- anything that gets in the way.

Daft slogans of pietistic vacuity that should not be on classroom walls

These slogans are often accompanied by photographs of wild animals in tame poses, cute cartoons, inspiring sunsets and noble buildings. Some are downright lies. Some are like candy floss, tasty at first, then suddenly empty. Some are there on the wall merely for a chance rhyme or alliteration. Here are some:

○ Stand up for what is right, even if you stand on your own.
○ Don't be a fool, learning's cool.

This shows a desperate and ingratiating longing to use the kids' (yeah, the kids') lingo. (Yeah, lingo.)

○ Never, never, never give up.
○ You have never lost until you quit trying.

I wanted to ask the teacher: So you have never given up or quit trying?

○ What you are begins with what you do.

It begins, in fact, with something your parents do.

○ Everyone is your friend.

This is a lie.

And more . . .

○ It is better to be beaten trying than to win by lying.

This is only there because of the banal rhyme. So much of this junk is like bad advertising.

○ Respect is not agreeing with everyone. It's agreeing that it's okay to disagree.
○ Life is a great big canvas, and you should throw all the paint on it that you can.
○ Success: don't just wish for it, work for it.
○ If you want to change the world, change your attitude.

Oh yeah?

○ A big journey begins with a little step.
○ Positive people don't put others down.
○ Open a book, open your mind.
○ Have you exercised your brain today?

If you are inspired by these, or think your children might be, go for it. Or go 4 it. But you are probably reading the wrong book.

The Subjects

L I S T 41   Poets to read to children

- Charles Causley
  He sings, and tells the truth, and surprises with the strange perfection of his imagery: Herod's hair 'as white as gin', for example. Read 'Mary Mary Magdalene' once, and you will never forget it. Nor will the children. *Collected Poems for Children* (Macmillan).

- Ted Hughes
  His poetry comes from the roots of England. You could teach simile with one poem, 'The Warm and the Cold' *Season Songs* (Faber).

- John Mole
  Delicate, and yet strong, he is not afraid to explore dangerous areas, like marital discord seen from the child's point of view. *The Conjuror's Rabbit* (Blackie), *Boo to a Goose* and *The Mad Parrot's Countdown* (Peterloo), *The Wonder Dish* (OUP).

- Lewis Carroll
  'The Walrus and the Carpenter' and 'You are old, Father William' from the Alice books still have power to provoke thought and to amuse.

- John Agard
  Direct and funny, he has the authentic rhythms of the speech of children. *I din do nuttin* (Magnet), *Laughter is an Egg* (Puffin).

- Kit Wright
  Makes them laugh, makes them think, makes them feel, gives pleasure. What more do you want? *Rabbiting On, Great Snakes!, Cat among the Pigeons, Hot Dog and Other Poems* (Puffin and Viking).

- Christina Rossetti
  Writes about the hottest subjects, the death of a child, for example. Author of some telling phrases: 'a breast full of milk'; 'My baby has a neck in creases'; 'What are deep? The ocean and truth'.

Rhymes that give innocent pleasure, and which encourage reading and pronunciation

These are counting out rhymes:

○ Eeny feeny figgery feg
  Deely dyly ham and egg
  Calico back and stony rock
  Arlum barlum bash!

○ Hoky poky winky wum
  How do you like your taties done?
  Snip snap snorum
  Hi popalourum
  Kate go scratch it
  You are OUT!

This is a little anonymous poem:

○ Elsie Marley's grown so fine
  She won't get up to feed the swine
  But stays in bed till eight or nine
  Lazy Elsie Marley!

This is a nonsense rhyme:

○ Have you ever ever ever
  In your long-legged life
  Seen a long-legged sailor
  With a long-legged wife?

  No I've never never never
  In my long-legged life
  Seen a long-legged sailor
  With a long-legged wife.

This is a clapping rhyme:

○ My boyfriend's name is Tony
  He comes from Macaroni
  With a pimple on his nose
  And two black toes
  And this is how my story goes:

One day he brought me peaches
One day he brought me pears
One day he brought me fifty francs
And kissed me on the stairs.

One day I was out walking
I saw my boyfriend talking
To a pretty little girl
With a pretty little curl
And this is what I did:

I threw back his peaches
And I threw back his pears
I threw back his fifty francs
And kicked him down the stairs.

Things children learn about when they make art

- Themselves – their personalities, their passions, their likes, their dislikes, their hopes, their fears. Art makes them reflect on themselves. It moves them towards self-awareness.
- The world about them – their environment, geographically and historically. It helps to make them tolerant of difference.
- The relationship between themselves and who, and what, is around them.

As I once wrote in an unfinished PhD thesis, 'Every work of art is a little research project into the difference between me and the rest of the world.'

- The medium of that art, whether it is line, pattern, clay, wood, paint, words, dance or musical notes.
- How to intensify their use of their senses.
- What 'beauty' is. Well, it is a beginning.

Only a little list, I admit – but full of truth and passion.

The benefits of drawing

Drawing is an underestimated activity. And it is useful not just in art, but in all the other subjects.

○ 'Taking a line for a walk' (as Paul Klee called it) is composed of 'lines into knowledge' (Klee again) and it 'calms and sensitizes the mind' (Maurice Rubens). That is why, at a low level, some of us doodle in boring or distressing meetings.
○ It encourages concentration.
○ It helps us to see, and seeing comes before words. We know this from looking at the curiosity in the eyes of very young babies.

I stood behind a young mother in the fish and chip shop tonight, and her baby daughter gazed at me for minutes over the young woman's shoulder as the latter paid for her family's dinner. I tried to make her smile, by smiling at her. She was just gazing: gazing, looking and learning.

○ It prolongs the looking at, and therefore the learning about, objects. It is all too easy to look without seeing. Drawing makes us see.
○ It transcends subject boundaries. Use drawing in science, for example: close observation of insects, engine parts.

Five rules for drawing

○ Use your pencil (or other graphic tool, ball point, charcoal, chalk, felt-tip pen) in as many different ways as you can. Use the point (obviously); the side of the lead; draw heavy and dark, and light; cross-hatch; smudge; combine all or some of these.

○ Make a decision about what kind of paper you are going to use; and whether you are going to use it landscape-wise or portrait-wise.

○ Draw your subject close-up.

This is to encourage large-scale, detailed drawing, and inclusion of details. It is better to say 'close-up' rather that 'big', because the former is a valid term: in photography for example.

○ No erasers! Wrong lines are interesting.

Giacometti's drawings are exemplary here.

○ Keep looking at your subject. Look, as Blake tells us we should, 'until it hurts'. As Monet stared at colour.

LIST 46   Displaying children's work: some principles

Skill in display is an important tool in any primary school teacher's kit. As Peter Dixon has written, the principles of good display can be seen any day on the front page of the *Sun* newspaper.

○ Keep it simple.
○ Be bold.

If the subject of the display is the circle, get a tractor wheel, or a tyre, or a wheel trim (you can find the last scattered on the verges of roads) to draw attention to the mathematics, and to mathematics' connection to life. If the subject is the sea, get a net, and those glass balls that weigh a net down. Spill some sand around. Have a tape playing of waves crashing on a shore: the aural element to display is almost always ignored.

○ Observe horizontals and verticals: avoid jaunty angles.
○ Also avoid unnecessary borders, especially the curly corrugated kind available, for some daft reason, from every County Supplies.
○ Change displays often. Nobody looks at one when it has been up more than a month.

More on display

o Teach the children to display their work.

Ask them: what will make people look at this display? What colours will command attention? How can we be sure that everyone in the class has some work here?

o Do not drape old curtains around displays.
o Never spend more time, effort and cost in the display of something than you and the children spent in the teaching and learning of it. What matters? The learning? Or the show? Eh? Well? Speak up, boy.
o All subjects, not just art, are served by good display.
o Display should reflect
  1. the ethnic make-up of your class. Poems in Swedish, for example, could be on the wall if you have a Swedish child in your class, and
  2. the ethnic make-up of the world.
o The main component of any display should be children's work, not commercially produced posters. You are aiming to make the room the children's environment, not the Oxford University Press's. When did you last see a child reading a poster labelled ANGLO-SAXON AND VIKING INVADERS? Or THE SIX WIVES OF HENRY VIII?
o Try to get a three-dimensional element in most displays.
o Include information for parents about the display: they might like to know what you are doing, and why.

Teachers sometimes assume that parents are passive clients of their children's schooling. Sometimes they are. But are you (assuming you're a parent) a passive client of your children's schooling?

In all the following subjects, remember their aesthetic element.

LIST 48

Reasons why music should be close to the centre of the curriculum

Over the last twenty-odd years, governments have relegated Music to non-league status. This is because, like Philosophy or Classics in universities, it does not contribute to the economy. Those who do not understand St Paul's truth that 'the love of money is the root of all evil' let such subjects wither. But here are the reasons:

❍ It gives pleasure, or offers children the possibility of joy.

Pleasure! Joy! These are unfashionable, innocent words surrounded by whorish words, words that'll do whatever you like for money – 'cost-effectiveness' and 'accountability', for example. But my words represent permanent and beautiful things, not ephemeral and ugly ones.

❍ It is therapeutic.

Kingsley Amis wrote somewhere that singing in a choir gave him more sensual pleasure than anything else except sex.

❍ Reading music helps with other kinds of reading, for example, reading words, reading numerical symbols, reading scientific symbols, reading art, reading maps.

The conductor Simon Rattle made this point when music was being sidelined by the strictures of the National Curriculum.

❍ It aids concentration aurally, much as drawing aids concentration visually, and dance aids concentration on the body and the space around it, and drama aids concentration on (among other things) social realities.

❍ It makes children aware of sounds, not just musical sounds, but also, to take three examples, birdsong, the human voice and the noise waves make when they suck back over pebbles on foreign shores.

❍ It encourages attention to detail.

❍ It enables performance, which gives confidence.

It can be a performance to a fellow-musician, or to a sympathetic friend.

❍ It is practical and tactile: the child is handling an instrument: violin, guitar, percussion. Or it may be the voice.

PE

All PE and games lessons should contain:

○ a warming up and what is ridiculously called in football a warming down;
○ a period of vigorous movement when the children's heartbeats are raised.
○ Link PE with health education.

Before and after exercise, see if they can find their pulses, and measure them. Link PE with Maths by asking them to find ways to show their findings (graphs and the like).

○ PE is about awareness of the body, awareness of the space around it, and awareness of the ways in which it balances.
○ The aesthetic element in PE is about the beauty of the human body in its movement and balance.

Be aware of this beauty. Keep the children aware of it: make them watch each other.

○ Link PE with art, by getting them to draw themselves and each other after a lesson in the gym.
○ Link PE with English, by getting them to talk about each other's movements
○ and by getting them to write about them.
○ Link PE with Science. The human body is a primary source.

Books, CDs and television programmes, on the other hand, are all secondary ones. Do some biological science, about the muscles and the bones, for example, after – or, better, during – a PE lesson.

Maths: two neglected principles

○ Help children to see the practical importance of Maths by taking them out and looking for shapes in the environment: rectangular windows, for example. Get them to photograph these shapes.

○ Link Maths with Art by noting, for example, the beauty of symmetry, and by building this into Art lessons. Get them to notice the presence of pattern in Mathematics and all the arts: rhyme and metre in poetry, repeated tunes in Music, repeated motifs in a William Morris print.

As G.H. Hardy has written, 'There is no permanent place in the world for ugly mathematics.'

LIST 51 Some enjoyable activities in mathematics: for younger children

These are not about mental arithmetic, but about learning how to think, reason and play with numbers.

Circle games

○ 'Today we will look silently round the circle, counting in ones, starting at twenty.' [Pause – a minute?] 'If I say twenty, who will say twenty-five? Thirty? What number will James say?' [Or, later,] 'Today we are counting back in tens ... who will say twenty-five, or fifteen ...?'

○ 'What shall we count today? The bricks in the tower? The panes of glass in those windows? The number of dogs in this picture? The children in the class? The tiles on the ceiling?' (Note that these are things the children can't touch, so it takes practice.)

○ Number series. You start off, 2, 4, 6 ... or 1, 3, 5 ... or 30, 27, 24 ... depending on how developed your class's understanding is. Then say: 'Hands up if you know the next number', or 'Say it if I point to you'. Then ask: 'What was the rule for that sequence?'

Activities for older children

Big numbers, and how to read them

Children love big numbers, and playing with them. One child asked me, 'What is the last number before infinity?' I suspect that thinking about big numbers gives some children a dizzying illusion of power.

Ask them: can you read this number: 987,654,321? They almost certainly can't. Say 'I'll show you how in five minutes. And how to read up to a billion!' Laurie Rousham, who gave me this activity, as well as all the others in this section, says to the children: 'Whose fault will it be if you can't say that number in ten minutes?' The children almost always assume it will be theirs. 'No!' says Laurie. 'It will be my fault!'

Write on the board the smallest and largest three-digit numbers (100 and 999). Ask them to read them. Then, tell them 'You must know the names of the commas. This time I'll write. You read':

1

21

321

4,321

'This is the first comma. It means "thousands". Say 4,321 to me.' Explain that by convention, we say the word 'thousand' in the singular. You go on to write the following numbers, and get the children to read each one, saying 'thousands' where the comma is.

54,321

654,321

until

7,654,321

This is the second comma. It means 'millions'. What does it say? Seven million, six hundred and fifty-four thousand, three hundred and twenty-one.

What's the next number? And so on to 987,654,321. That's what I ask you to read! And you can!

Put a number in front of it, with its comma:

8,987,654,321

What does that '8' mean, in that position?

There is no clear and simple answer to this question. In the UK nowadays this 8 normally stands for 'billions', in line with the American definition; but care is needed because some people still cling to the old definitions, holding that 1,000,000,000 is a milliard and that a British billion is 1,000,000,000,000.

○ What's my rule? I am going to call this 'Laurie's Game'. Establish that rules can have two parts, for example, 'If it's odd, add 3; if it's even, halve it.' 'Give me a number':

52 > 26 > 13 > 18 > 9 > 12 > 6 > 3 > 6 > 3 > 6 > 3 and so on ... (it will be seen that the last four numbers form a loop)

There are only two loops! All numbers go into either the sequence above, or into 4 > 2 > 1 > 4. Try it with 97:

97 > 100 > 50 > 25 > 28 > 14 > 7 > 10 > 5 > 8 > 4 > 2 > 1 > 4 > 2 > 2 > 1 ... and so on

Think of what's going on in the children's brains here, the thinking and the learning. When you teach this lesson, the excitement about numbers is palpable.

And some more!

Considering statements

Debate with the children: some statements are matters of opinion ('Arsenal is better than Manchester United') and others are, for all practical purposes, matters of fact. Ask the children to think individually, and then to discuss in groups whether these statements are always true, sometimes true, or never true. Or 'iffy', as Laurie puts it. Whatever they are, they are not matters of opinion. This helps children to reason.

Multiplying by positive numbers makes positive numbers larger. Always true, sometimes true, or never true?

$3 \times 7 = 21$
$5 \times 8 = 40$
but $\frac{1}{2} \times 8 = 4$
and $1 \times 1 = 1$

so sometimes true.

A four-sided shape with two parallel sides is a parallelogram. This is sometimes true: a trapezium also has two parallel sides, and is not a parallelogram.

If you increase a price by 10 per cent and then decrease it by 10 per cent, you will return to the original price. The statement is false, because the second 10 per cent is the percentage of the new price. Say the old price was £12, the new price is £13.20, the third price will be £11.88.

The sum of two numbers is the same as its product:
Rarely true: $2 \times 2 = 4$, $2 + 2 = 4$. But $3 + 3 = 6$, $3 \times 3 = 9$

Triangles tessellate. This is always true.

The centrality of science

○ Science, in its own special way, can help us to understand our world. Children should be encouraged to ask questions about their environment from an early age.

○ If you are biased towards the arts, it is worth remembering the role of science in making books, paint, musical instruments and so on.

○ Science affects everybody, including poets, musicians, engineers, teachers, doctors and athletes. Get the children to think about how science directly affects them.

○ Science isn't all about right and wrong answers. If scientists hadn't used their minds creatively, they wouldn't have discovered electricity, penicillin or the concept of gravity.

○ Science has improved people's lives. Think about vaccines for serious illnesses, such as TB, polio, smallpox and tetanus; think about fresh food in your fridge, hot showers, clean clothes and comfortable beds.

○ Get children to think about how science helps them through the day. Where has the food they've eaten come from? How have their clothes been made? How have images appeared on the TV screen?

○ Encourage them to think of further ways their day could be improved. Perhaps one of their inventions will change the world for future generations.

○ Think about Space, and how Earth is the only planet in the solar system the right distance from the sun to support intelligent life.

Geography: working with maps

This subject, like charity, begins at home, with the question, 'Where am I in the world?'

Ask the children to draw a map of

- their bedroom
- their classroom
- their school
- their town or area of the town, or their village
- their perfect island

Ask them, what would be a good symbol on a map for

- a copse of trees
- a traffic island
- a McDonald's restaurant

The atlas game, or our journey to the IT room

Ask the children to write a poem composed of alliterating lines, like this:

We journeyed joyfully to Japan
We danced dangerously into Denmark

where the verb, the adverb and the country all begin with the same sound (not necessarily the same letter, of course). When they have a poem of, say, fifteen lines, get them to arrange the lines in an order that is geographically feasible, putting, for example, lines like

We flew ferociously into France

next to

We spiralled speedily into Spain.

If they do this on computers, using cut and paste, they are learning in the following subjects: Geography, IT, literacy, poetry.

Media studies: some principles

- ○ Children should study media critically. Courses should verge on scepticism.
- ○ The aesthetic here is in the study of the beauty (or otherwise) of form, colour, pattern, etc. – in advertisements, for example.
- ○ This study should include work on: advertisements, magazines, newspapers, packaging, radios, television, videos and DVDs.
- ○ They should discuss the ways that the media affect them.
- ○ They should consider the way technology does what it does.

How are emails different from phone calls, texts and letters? What are the effects of these differences? How do adverts on television, in the press, in adverts, on hoardings, over the shops, differ?

- ○ They should make media.

Children should be given the power to be behind the camera, for example, as well as in front of it.

- ○ They should be involved not only in writing but also in publishing their work.

History: some important features of history in the classroom

○ The best beginning for the teaching of history is local history.

What about a history of the house or flat they live in? Or their high street. All towns have books of old photographs that provide evidence.

○ History is enjoyable because it is made up of stories.

Narrative is important to all of us. Even apocryphal stories in history – Alfred and the cakes, the adventures of Robin Hood – matter because they speak of the roots of our society, or of our communal beliefs about it. And they have an aesthetic component.

○ History is not objective fact.

This is not only because so many facts are hidden or lost, but because when anyone writes anything, they write it from their position. It is 'distillation of rumour' (Carlyle).

An exercise: cause a strange event to happen in the classroom: the TA comes in and picks a fight with you, or is dressed as an admiral and goes around the room doing sea-dog things, or drags a toy animal after her on a length of string, talking to it. Then, next day, ask the children to write an account of what happened, getting all the details in. Compare the accounts.

○ The use of artefacts.

The art of a former time teaches much about that time. Also, artefacts provide a basis for evidence-based learning, and for aesthetic appreciation.

○ The use of visits.

More evidence-based learning. Blank notebooks are best for visits, with instructions that children should look, listen, write and draw all day long.

Religious Education: the aesthetic

○ Children should have opportunities to look at religious art from all traditions.

They can, for example, compare the art of Islam (empty of human forms) with the art of Christianity (full of them).

○ Religions are full of the aesthetic quality of narrative.
○ In the UK, children have a unique opportunity to look at great Norman, Early English, Perpendicular and Decorated religious architecture.

I was in a Durham school once. The children had never been taken to the cathedral. A primary source for Norman history, RE and Art (the nave is the finest Norman construction) had been ignored in favour of hack history books.

○ What about writing prayers?
○ One No-no-no-please-stop-it-NOW! on the RE/aesthetics front is the nativity play written by Sir or Miss and acted by children with towelling round their heads while a choir sings 'Little Donkey' and 'Mary's Boy Child' and a blonde Mary dressed in blue holds a plastic doll in her arms and Joseph gazes adoringly at them both and extras dressed as kings and shepherds gaze adoringly too at the plastic doll.

I don't feel well, just typing this.

LIST 59   The world's main living religions

In order from the oldest to the youngest, with brief notes on the religions that teachers are likely to come across in the classroom.

(Sources: *The Illustrated Encyclopaedia of World Religions*, general editor Chris Richards (Element), *The Concise Encyclopaedia of Living Faiths*, editor R.C. Zaehner (Hutchinson).

Hinduism

is, of course, linked with the country and people of India. It's concerned with what believers do more than with what they believe. It's about five thousand years old, and it has the third largest number of adherents. It does not seek converts. Critical terms: Brahman is ultimate reality. Samsara is the cycle of birth and rebirth. Karma: good actions have a good reaction, bad ones a bad one.

Judaism

is the oldest of the monotheistic religions (meaning that its adherents believe in a single God). It is four thousand years old. Like Islam and Christianity, it is a religion of the book, and its central text is the Torah, the first five books of the Old Testament. Orthodox Jews interpret it almost literally; Conservative and Reformed less so. This distinction between conservative and liberal runs through all religions.

Buddhism

is 2,500 years old. It is not necessarily deistic (believing in God, or gods): it is, indeed, possible to be an atheist Buddhist. It sets out essentials truths: all life involves suffering (dukkha). This is caused by selfish craving. We must solve the problem, not the symptoms, by finding wisdom, following the Eightfold Path of Buddhism.

Jainism

began in the fifth century BCE. It believes in non-violence (Ahisma). Jain comes from a word meaning self-control. These are the two things that lead to salvation.

61

Christianity

Two thousand years old. The central facts for Christianity are the birth of Christ, his cross and his empty tomb. For all Christians, redemption is through Christ, however we interpret all the main words in that sentence (Christians, redemption, Christ). There are, of course, divisions between the Catholic tradition, the Orthodox and the Protestant. Conservative and liberal are two other divisions that cut across the other set, analogous to Orthodox and liberal in Judaism. Again, much of it concerns interpretation of the scriptures.

Islam

Although the prophet Mohammed was the last of the prophets, and though to the rest of the world, Islam ('peace') started with him, Muslims believe that all the prophets, from Adam onwards, were obedient to God, and therefore were Muslims.

Most Muslims are Sunni, about 80 per cent. The largest other group is composed of Shi'ite Muslims. The differences between them stem from beliefs about who succeeded the prophet after his death.

Sikhism

The common surname for men ('Singh') and for women ('Kaur') speaks of an interest in opposing a system in which people could be identified by their surnames as being of a particular caste. Sikhs set much store by the idea of hospitality, especially in their gurdwara, their place of worship.

LIST 60 Personal, Social and Moral Education: some principles

In this area, which would be a sound basis for the whole curriculum – it is, after all, about me, the world and everything else – there are basic principles:

○ The more controversial a subject, the more likely it is to help the children learn.
○ Therefore, it must include subjects that are often taboo in the classroom: family breakdown, serious illness and death are three examples.

And it should allow the possibilities of discussing these things before they become critical, when a child's family breaks up, for example, or a parent becomes ill or someone dies.

○ It is about justice and injustice.

It can address wider issues that have an impact on individual children, for example, sexism, racism and other prejudices.

○ It is about safety.

Not merely in the relatively limited sense of keeping children safe, but in the wider and more powerful one of teaching them how to keep themselves safe.

○ It cannot be taught in a formal way, 'delivered' in modern jargon: it constantly requires talk on the part of pupils.

PSME across the subjects

If they are taught properly, all subjects teach PSME. For example, a child is doing PSME when she

- looks into her own experience and feelings for the purpose of writing a poem or a story.
- draws an old person from life.
- collaborates in a scientific experiment.
- cooks a meal.
- helps a child who has fallen over.
- organizes a game in which she has to work with friends towards a common objective.
- sings or plays a musical instrument in a group.
- plays the mental arithmetic games in my maths section with friends.

Part of PSME should be concerned with finding out what children think and feel at school.

Emotional maps. Ask the children to draw a map of the school, with sentences on it about each area, about how they feel about it and what they do there. For example, in the hall: I feel happy when I do PE ... At assembly time, I feel bored ... In the toilet, we gossip about school ... I like sitting under the stairs because it is quiet there ...

It is useful to have drawn your own emotional map first.

Questions children ask about sex, or would ask if they had a chance to do it without embarrassing themselves or you

Part of PSME is Sex Education. It is, of course, notoriously difficult to teach, and this is exacerbated by the fact that social mores about sex change with remarkable speed. For example, it was easy, forty years ago, to talk about the two-parent family with two children as if it were immutable reality.

It is all very well to say that 'school answers questions about sex as they arise'; but is the ethos in the school amenable to the questions being raised?

In one school, the teachers provided a box into which Year 6 children could drop slips of paper with questions about sex. The teachers made it clear that any questions were allowed. The box was there for a long time. What follows is what they asked. I have categorized the questions.

Questions requiring information at a low level

- What is a nipple?
- What are stretch marks?
- What are pubic hairs?
- How does the male seed get inside the body?
- Can you go swimming when you are wearing a pad?
- How does the stomach swell up on a female?
- What are sex organs?

Questions, sometimes informed by anxiety, requiring information at a higher level

- What are the signs of starting your periods?
- If you are gay do you have to use a condom?
- How do you know if you have got AIDS?
- Where does the milk come from?
- Do you usually start your periods just before your mum started them?
- Why are babies smaller when there are more of them, e.g. twins are usually bigger than triplets?

65

- On some TV programmes, when two people are making love they make noises. Why is that?
- How do women's breasts produce milk?

Questions reflecting serious worries or misunderstandings

- Why is it that sometimes the mother dies in childbirth?
- What causes a miscarriage?
- Why does the baby come out sometimes when they aren't ready?
- Why do you get Siamese twins?

That is what the child wrote. The correct term these days is, of course, 'conjoined twins'.

- What happens if the woman gets cancer? Does the baby get it?

Questions exposing grave misunderstanding

- How does a man know, say, if they wanted twins, whether he has to send two sperms in?
- How long does it take to make a baby?
- If the woman is pregnant and they didn't know and they had sex again what will happen to the baby?

(From *Personal, Social and Moral Education*, Fred Sedgwick (David Fulton).) Thanks again to Kexborough Primary School, Barnsley.

Citizenship

Some ideas

○ Get the children to look around the classroom and plan improvements.

Let groups implement their plans, one each half term. Give them a budget.

○ If there isn't one already, set up a school's council.

It should be empowered to discuss issues like bullying, development of the site and racism.

○ Debate lessons.

Some subjects: hunting, the roles of the sexes in the home, the place of the car vis-à-vis public transport.

○ Bring in outside speakers from the community.
○ Help the children to run a school magazine.
○ Use role play to explore the dynamics of society.
○ Help children to write rules for behaviour.
○ Run a healthy schools programme.

LIST 65 Ways of improving work with computers

- If you have an IT suite, you should also have two or three computers in your classroom, so that they are seen by the children as everyday tools, like pens and pencils.
- Children should compose stories, poems, reports, etc. on them, not type up fair copies.

In here is a general rule. Children writing should behave as much as possible like professional writers. The latter do not scribble away, rubbing out occasionally, putting their hands up when they are unable to spell something or need another piece of paper, and, when they are satisfied with the result, 'type it up on the computer'. They *compose* on the computer.

- Develop an email relationship with another school.

Best of all, develop a relationship with a school in another country, another continent, another planet.

- Using the internet.

Get the children to compare the quality of information they receive from it with what they get from books. Get them to identify the advantages and disadvantages of each (up-to-dateness; reliability).

Ways of making children laugh

Jokes for children shouldn't be jokes just for children. As with poems, a real joke is a joke that appeals to all. Jokes and poems that are good for children are good for adults. Some jokes (or poems) merely have frames of reference narrower than that of other jokes or poems.

○ Remember, if you have a sense of humour, they will respond to it. If you are open with them, they will be open with you.

○ Be aware that, to the children, you are sometimes unintentionally funny. Be prepared to laugh at yourself.

○ Tell children about events from your childhood. You will seem human to them, even if you aren't.

○ Collect playground rhymes with the children, their parents and your colleagues.

Get a copy of *The Lore and Language of Schoolchildren* by Opie and Opie. Also, by the same authors, *The Singing Game* (both OUP).

○ Keep in touch with the children's culture: TV, films, toys, so that you can share jokes about it.

However you feel, don't be superior about it. As with so much in teaching, it is useful to remember your own schooling: recall your enthusiasms as a child: Barbie dolls, transformers, football stickers and, going back a while, cigarette cards. But don't use their language – they hate it!

LIST 67

And of sharing other kinds of pleasure

○ Surprise children.

Many lessons in the arts, especially, can be introduced with the sentence 'Now we are going to do something wicked/naughty'. For example, in drama, 'Today we are going to steal apples from an orchard'; in writing, 'we are going to write a poem entirely made up of lies'. Or, we are going to write a poem made up of insults, inspired by Shakespeare's amazing variety: 'Thou map of woe ... base bondsman ... execrable dog ...' Or of boasts. Or get them to write stories about naughty things they did when they were young.

○ Take as many lessons as you can in the open air, or in any non-school building.

In a church, enable them to learn RE, History, English, Art and Architecture, simply by looking hard. The same applies to museums and art galleries. And to less elevated places: town centres, bingo halls, football grounds.

○ Peter Dixon (in his book *Trespassers*) has a picture of a teacher telling her class 'We are going to begin our topic about the Egyptians by watching Liz Taylor clasping the asp to her bosom and after that we will be embalming some fish I've brought to school'. A boy is thinking 'This sounds better that palm trees, irrigation and pyramids'. A point brilliantly made. All topics have a way in like this ...

Other topics with surprises

○ Ancient Rome?

How about a video of that moment in *Carry on Cleo* when Kenneth Williams, playing Caesar at the moment of his assassination, cries 'Infamy! Infamy! They've all got it in for me!'

○ The Myself topic?

A collection of locks of hair, or toenail parings, each in a matchbox, and carefully labelled, will attractively offset the pretty baby photos.

○ India and the subcontinent?

Give every child, as the topic begins, half of one of those poppadoms that have bits of chilli in. At first, they will taste the bland, crisp flavour; and then, simultaneously, they will all gasp and complain, and reach for the milk (better than water at negating chilli heat) you have thoughtfully provided. Great fun, this. Have a camera ready. 'This is Jonathan eating a bit of chilli' will have interest on the wall longer than the elements in many displays.

Features of official assessment methods (Sats)

○ They are quantitative. That is, concerned with numbers.
○ They are administrative and political in their aims.
○ They are insensitive to human realities.

Children's emotions and children's backgrounds (and teachers' emotions and teachers' backgrounds) do not matter.

○ They assume predetermined learning outcomes: levels and the like.
○ They are purely summative: entirely concerned with the outcomes of tests.
○ The tests happen outside the context of learning – at times, for example, when the classroom is silent, and discourse banned.
○ Their administrators tacitly assume that learning, and, indeed, being a human being, is a simple matter.

Features of humanistic assessment methods

○ They are qualitative.
○ They are educational rather than administrative or political.
○ They admit and wrestle with complexities.
○ They are ongoing.

Teachers assess in a humane way, all the time, and that assessment contributes something to their teaching.

○ They try to see the growth of understanding ...
○ ... therefore, they are complex and time-consuming.
○ They admit of learning not anticipated by the teacher (or, more seriously, the system).
○ They are part of the learning process.
○ They are open to emotional realities. (See *Assessing Children's Learning*, by Mary Jane Drummond (David Fulton).)

Difficulties with Children

4

LIST 71   Ways of inflaming a situation

○ Confront all misdemeanours, no matter how trivial.

This is called 'zero tolerance', also 'manic vigilance'. Whatever it is called, it is a recipe for trouble. Imagine it in a marriage, and you'll see what I mean. 'You've washed up, darling, but what about this spoon? No sugar in your coffee for a week.'

○ Always up the ante.

Use your innate sense of moral indignation to humiliate the miscreant further. Always remember, you are perfect. If, for example, you are upbraiding a child for swearing, you must behave as if you are sure you have never sworn in your life. If this is true, you have either never vacuumed the stairs, or changed the duvet cover. Or else you are a saint.

○ Paint the child into a corner.

It is so satisfying to see a child lost for words because of anger and guilt. As a teacher once said to me, without irony, 'They don't like it when you humiliate them.'

○ Encourage children to spy on each other.

I was in a school where 'monitors' wrote the names of 'naughty' children on the blackboard. The monitors were little more than what used to be called 'coppers' narks'.

More ways to wind them up

○ Use 'assertive' discipline, and show you expect the worst.

'Yesterday your behaviour was appalling and today I expect better' means 'Yesterday your behaviour was appalling and today I don't hold out much hope of an improvement', and the children (and you) know it.

○ Constantly raise your voice.

You are so attractive when you shout, or when your voice is, as Edward Blishen puts it, 'on squeaking tiptoe'.

○ Use aggressive language, especially sarcasm.
○ Use denigration of the child's personality: 'That's just what I would expect from you.'

'You poisonous little oaf' is left unsaid, of course, but it is equally well understood by each party.

○ Because, as a teacher, you are, by that fact, middle-class, constantly be aware of the failings of people less elevated than you.

Express your superiority with your accent, and your greater verbal fluency.

Ways of taking the heat out

○ Be as calm as you can. Long breaths help.
○ Make the child understand that you know why he is angry.
○ Respect everyone, even children who are behaving badly.

They are human beings made in the image of God. 'Respect' has always been bandied as something vital for children to show teachers. It cuts both ways.

○ Behave as though you expect decent behaviour, even when, or especially when, this is difficult because of what the child did, or is rumoured to have done, last week, last month, last year, or when she was in the infants.
○ Make your default voice a quiet one.

Shout once a year, and that only for safety's sake. 'Get down from there! Now!'

○ Offer the child time out with a TA to calm down.
○ Do not give children the chance to ferment their grudge by putting them outside the head's office for lunchtime, so that everyone can see that they've been naughty.

Symptoms of low self-esteem in children

or, for that matter, with appropriate changes, in adults (adapted from *Windows on our Children*, Violet Oaklander).

- They need, above all else, to win.
- They need to be perfect.

In the arts and the sciences, recognition that perfection is either a long way off, or unattainable, is essential. So is the opposite – mess, mistakes, crossings-out ...

- They brag.
- They give away money or sweets.

Here the child is currying favour.

- They seek attention.
- They tease.
- They blame others for everything.

Here the child is trying to advance his self-esteem by lowering that of others.

- They are over self-critical.
- They make excuses constantly.
- They are always apologizing.

Here the child is warding off criticism – perhaps he has had too much of it in the past?

- They are frightened of trying new things.
- They show anxiety in new situations.

Some of these symptoms seem to contradict others. On the other hand, that seems to be the nature of being a human being. As Walt Whitman wrote: 'Do I contradict myself? / Very well then I contradict myself ...'

L I S T 75   Dealing with bullying

The school's, and your classroom's, first requirement here is a climate in which bullying is seen for what it is, unacceptable.

○ Identify those likely to be bullied, but be aware that some children not so identified may be bullied.
○ Show that you value those you have identified as likely to be bullied, without helping bullies identify them as such.
○ Note danger times, especially lunchtime with Midday Supervisory Assistants (MDSAs) on duty.
○ Keep the MDSAs aware of your thinking and findings about bullies in the school, while insisting on confidentiality (these people are often parents and neighbours of the children).
○ Identify those likely to be bullies, and work to improve their self-esteem in the classroom.
○ Give likely bullies responsibilities, thus making it clear that you expect good things of them.
○ Never bully children.

Someone is going to say, 'How can he write that? Teachers never bully children these days.' That person is a sentimentalist. There is no physical cruelty any more, because it is outlawed, but there is mental cruelty.

Modern idiocies to be resisted

○ No animals allowed in the classroom for the sake of avoiding catching AIDS from the hamster or hepatitis B from the rabbit.

This is sad because, first, most children love animals, and second, and more importantly, because they learn from them. They learn about the animals themselves, their relationship with them, and how to look after them. These animals are scientifically and emotionally valuable.

And we should have animals in classrooms because they teach children, in a relatively painless way, about death. This is impossible to teach in any other way, except during crises, or with good literature.

○ No playing conkers in the autumn.
○ No playing snowballs in the winter.
○ No sliding on the ice.

These three rules seem to fly in the face of what it is to be a child in the UK. What else are conkers, snow and ice for? The reasons for these prohibitions are not, chiefly, the safety of the children, but the protection of the school's and the authority's back.

○ No goggles in swimming lessons.

I came across this rule in a school, and found confusing messages about it. One teacher had been adjusting a child's goggles, while another child had got into trouble in the water. Someone else said that goggles restricted vision.

Daft notions

There should be ...

○ No footballs on the playground.

I'm with anyone who restricts the influence of football on schools. A fragment of its jargon – league tables – has infected our practice. But what else are most of the boys, and some of the girls, to do?

○ No toilet roll insides, for fear of infection (not that toilet roll insides were much use anyway, used, as they were, to make identical Father Christmases).

When was a toilet roll inside ever infected with anything? I worry about the minds of some people.

○ No sand trays, they're dirty.

Of course they're dirty. Life, like the best jazz, *is* dirty. I've just read that babies exposed to infections are less likely to catch leukaemia. Children exposed to dirt in a sand tray are more likely to be healthy than children protected neurotically from that dirt.

○ No staple guns. They have been banned because they could be dangerous.

But they are vital for display. They should be kept securely.

○ No cotton wool. You might get little bits of it in your eye.

Fallacies

It is fallacious that these are good ideas:

○ No standing (this is for you, not the children) on chairs to reach for high things.
○ Security systems that would defend the Crown Jewels, and which leave visitors and parents fuming for minutes in the rain at the front door under a sign that says 'WELCOME TO BOG STREET SCHOOL'.

I promise you, the visitor urgently needs to write YOU'RE in big letters in front of those fatuous words.

Some idiocies are religious in origin

○ No mention of the body and blood of Christ, or of the Holy Ghost, because they might frighten children.

These strictures, from a local education authority, were later withdrawn. But they show how some minds work.

○ No books mentioning witches, or Hallowe'en.

This comes from the evangelical wing of Christianity, and those evangelicals explain it thus: this whole area is a possible doorway to harmful things, like Ouija boards and the occult. The dark side to spirituality is a reality, and children need to be protected from it. Meg and Mog as a corrupting pair seems far-fetched to me. And how are you going to teach *Macbeth* later on?

Assembly

○ Make sure your class gets into the hall at the accepted time.
○ Make sure they come in talking quietly.

What is the point of the silence rule? Do you walk into the staffroom silently? As I have written, child writers should behave as much as possible like the best professional writers. Similarly, child workers should behave like the best adult workers: you gossip as you prepare for work. Well, I do.

○ It's assembly. So everyone ought to be there, including the TAs.

It's like a sacrament, the learning parts of the school coming together.

○ Assembly should not be clogged up with administrative trivia.
○ And it should be short.
○ Music should be listened to, not used as a background.

(See my book *100 Ideas for Primary Assemblies*, published by Continuum.)

If you are taking assembly:

○ Be crisp in delivery and content.
○ Keep it short: never more than twenty minutes.

How would you like to sit on the floor for much longer, especially if – and I, having recently lost two stone in weight am serious about this – you have less padding on the bottom than some. I find hard chairs uncomfortable, and I feel sympathy for thin children in assembly.

○ If you use music, make it music that encourages reflection.

Never play fast rock or hot jazz, or 'The Ride of the Valkyries', and expect the children to sit still.

○ Say something brief about the music, or the composer/artist.

'Beethoven, who wrote this, was deaf and never heard it' ...
'Brahms used to get up at 5 o'clock every morning, and drink strong coffee and smoke a cigar before he started work' ...

○ Give them a task: 'Listen hard to this music, and find when the trumpet comes in ...' and questions: 'How many instruments can you hear?'
○ When it's time to stop the music, don't just click it off. Fade it out.
○ Compose an assembly of several different elements: a short story, a poem, a song, a prayer, a moment's silence, something to look at, something to listen to, something to smell (why not? a joss stick? hyacinths? lavender? incense?) rather than one long element.

If a child is bored by one part of your assembly, she may be engaged by another, and, even if she isn't, the change will be a minor relief anyway.

○ Involve children (well-rehearsed) wherever possible, reading their writing, or showing off their art, or their science, or their dance.
○ Don't preach.

If you have a message (and it is not compulsory) assume that some will get it, some won't and some will get part of it. Some won't get it now, but will in a minute, or maybe next Christmas, or maybe when they're grown up. Think of the parable of the sower.

○ Don't use assembly for football triumphalism.

The team that won yesterday afternoon get quite enough adulation from their dads and the football teacher.

Types of teacher

○ The restricted professional.

This teacher does the job in a basic way, but with no spark. Goes on courses, when told to. Copies, rather than develops, what s/he's taught on them. Doesn't notice what other teachers do. Develops tics in teaching and uses them 'because they work': shouting for silence, lining up children with a blow of a whistle, restricting the teaching of reading to phonics.

○ The extended professional.

This teacher also does the job, but is constantly looking for ways of improving practice. Goes on courses, and is often disappointed, or even angered, by them. Develops, rather than copies, ideas. Is interested in what other teachers do. Has understood that we wouldn't trust a doctor who didn't keep up and innovate. So there is no reason to trust a teacher that doesn't either.

○ The technician.

This person is a different animal in the classroom from what s/he is in the pub. Has to work on technique, because to act naturally would cause trouble. This is not necessarily a bad thing, because this teacher may well be constantly thinking about his or her work.

○ The natural.

Apart from the beer, the flirtation, the politics and the risqué jokes, what s/he is in the pub is what s/he is in the classroom. This has advantages, but it also has disadvantages. Perhaps this teacher would gain from work on technique.

○ The cynic.

Usually sits in the same chair in the staffroom every day. Has his or her own mug. Has been wherever you think it might be good for you and your class to go. It wasn't much good, and s/he doesn't recommend it.

The cynic

The cynic says:

- ○ In my last school, we used to ..., and it didn't work there ...
- ○ The kids round here aren't up to creativity ...
- ○ Children these days have too much done for them.
- ○ Your ideas might work at St Michael and All Angels, but here at Bog Street, they haven't a chance.

About a child who was misbehaving, one cynic said, 'Give her that reading book and tell her to copy out two pages. She'll hate that.'

It is enough to say that adults have been denigrating children since forever. Here is one example from, of all people, Socrates (469–399 BC): 'Children today love luxury too much. They have execrable manners, flout authority, have no respect for their elders ...' This is from Michael Rosen's *Penguin Book of Childhood*. Can it always have been true that children were so awful? Well, yes: from the point of view of the decrepit and jealous old.

Ways of leading Teaching Assistants (TAs)

Don't

○ get them slicing paper and putting up displays while you are teaching.

○ send them on errands for a cup of tea or anything else.

○ leave them with the responsibility of washing up in the staffroom.

○ confuse their disgracefully low pay with their worth.

Do

○ get them closely involved with what the children are doing.

○ give them observing and recording responsibilities: what's going on as you teach?

○ remember that they have experience and knowledge that you don't have. Tap into it.

○ remember that they often have interests (or hobbies, as they are rather drearily called) that can be usefully brought into the classroom: bread-making, clog-dancing, cookery, playing an instrument, reading, painting, drawing, singing, reading Jane Austen.

○ remember that although you are a teacher in a particular, professional sense, recognized by university or college, local authority and union, TAs do teacherly tasks every day.

Everything they do should be directed towards helping children to learn.

LIST 84
Leading Mid-Day Supervisory Assistants (MDSAs)

Persuade the headteacher to offer them a course when they are appointed, or at least written guidelines. There is advice that they need to be given, because it will not, necessarily, have come their way. Much of it is contained in List 71 'Ways of inflaming a situation' and List 73 'Ways of taking the heat out'. Also, they may need help with issues about discrimination.

What they need to know

○ Dealing with children in a school does not always follow the same principles as dealing with children at home.

For example, at home you can occasionally change rules, or bend them. You can indulge children, give them treats. These are out of order in the school lunch break.

The rest of the items on this list are as applicable at home as they are at school.

○ They should not show favouritism.
○ Shouting is rarely a good thing.
○ Moral indignation is a useful emotion when you are writing savage satirical poetry, but not when looking after children.

It takes up time, both now and at the end of your life.

○ It is good for children to get muddy.
○ There has to be a balance between safety and risk.

If MDSAs only worry about safety, much experience that children need will be missed.

Encouraging student teachers

They need to know:

○ Where's the toilet?
○ Where can they leave coats and other gear?
○ Can they choose any mug to drink from?

One student teacher told me about his mentor. His lecturer had arrived, and made a cup of coffee. The mentor grabbed the cup, poured its content down the sink and said that she was 'very particular about who used her cup'.

○ Can they choose any chair?
○ Can they be treated like colleagues?

After all, they are closer to the fount of wisdom than you are. I don't mean their college or university so much as their childhood: they come, as Wordsworth said, 'trailing clouds of glory'.

○ Make it clear: they are always welcome in the staffroom.
○ Induct them into the profession, in the examples of professionalism you set for them:
  – not criticizing colleagues, even the headteacher
  – not speaking disrespectfully of children and parents
  – not speaking disrespectfully of the student's college and their lecturers.

All too often, cynical teachers view these men and women with disdain: a bad attitude to convey to students.

What supply teachers need to know

○ Again, where's the toilet?
○ Can they, too, choose any mug to drink from, or any chair to sit in, or must they be careful?
○ Is there a child in the class with a medical condition?
○ Or a mental one?
○ Where is the basic equipment in your classroom?
○ The names of the children who need special treatment, for any number of reasons:

   Recent bereavement, dyslexia, Asperger's, autism, children who are sensitive, and anxious about change (especially in Reception).

○ Child protection issues: is there, for example, a child who must leave school with one named person only?

With the Parents

5

LIST 87 When writing reports

○ Keep a notebook throughout the year, and make sure that you jot notes on every child.

This makes the final report both less of a chore and more truthful. Make sure that these notes contain something positive about every child – little kindnesses, successful work.

○ Show that you have some appreciation of each child's character.
○ Avoid jargon about Sats and the like.

The parents may want to hear it, because they read the *Daily Mail*, and therefore think that the Sats and the league tables mean something. But you should serve them the truth, as you see it, about their child.

○ Write clearly.

See my advice from George Orwell about clear writing in List 16.

○ Don't be clever.

I once wrote on a football-mad boy's report (I cringe at the memory) 'Kevin has to learn that life is more than a midfield strategy.' That was disgraceful.

○ Remember that illegible signatures irritate parents.

Well, I'm a parent, and they irritate me.

○ Get the children to write a report on you.

Obviously, you'll point out how important it is to be encouraging. But honesty is required too. Use what they write in your talks with parents.

During parents' evenings

- ○ Understand that there are areas of knowledge that they have that you don't.
- ○ A list of things the parents know about their children that you don't:
  - – their fears
  - – their nightmares
  - – their joys
  - – what they're like on Christmas morning
  - – what they're like on holiday
  - – what they think of you
  - – what they think of school
- ○ Find out about expertise that they have, and get them into the classroom to share that expertise.
- ○ Don't underestimate them when they work alongside you and the children in the classroom (or outside it).
- ○ Involve parents in projects: collecting playground rhymes from their childhood, for example; using their memories of recent history.

From the child's point of view

I asked a group of children to write a short message to any teacher.

○ You taught me that learning is everything, friends are not.

○ You helped me through bad times, like when my mum and dad split up.

○ You taught me courage and belief and to make my own life up. You gave me freedom.

○ You taught me metaphor and similes. I still don't understand, only a bit.

○ I wrote as fast as I could but I could not write fast. You kept me in at lunchtime and it was unfair.

○ You showed me how to draw a realistic eye.

○ You taught me how to eat a Brussels sprout.

○ You held my hand when I had toothache.

○ You told me what to do in school dinners when it was my first day.

○ You helped me when I fainted.

○ You taught me how to walk through the Bible.

○ I flicked a bit of rubber across the room. You told me not to be silly, because it doesn't get you anywhere.

Some lies about teaching

○ Children from working-class homes are deficient in language.

See this given the lie in *Young Children Learning*, by Barbara Tizard and Martin Hughes, and *The Meaning Makers*, by Gordon Wells. Some of these children sometimes fail in *school* language, a very different matter from failing in language generally. They come to school with a hundred languages, and we take all of them away, except one.

○ Choice between schools is a good thing.

No. Parents don't want to choose between academies specializing in one subject or another. They want their local school to teach everything well.

○ Spelling, grammar and syntax are basic skills.

No again. Telling the truth through writing is a basic skill. Spelling, grammar and syntax are tools.

○ 'Literacy' encompasses 'language'.

In fact, the first of these words was not recorded until 1883. It was formed as an antithesis to 'illiteracy'. Its emphasis on phonics, phonemes and the rest (surviving to this day) is a ridiculous limitation of what language can do. Language enables thought. It can 'teach the free man how to praise' (W.H. Auden).

The same goes, with the relevant changes, for 'numeracy' and 'mathematics'.

LIST 91 Damned lies

○ Comprehensive schools can coexist with grammar schools.

Of course they can't: the grammar school in any area creams off pupils, making the comprehensive essentially what used to be called a secondary modern.

○ There was a progressive movement in the 1960s and 1970s which destroyed basic, formal education in primary schools and led to social unrest, drug addiction, teenage pregnancy and, potentially at least, to the end of civilization as we know it.

No there wasn't, and no it didn't. I was there, and almost all schools carried on with chalk-and-talk while a few lively ones imitated the snapshots in the Plowden Report. If there is social unrest, drug addiction and teenage pregnancy today, it is the responsibility of the formal teaching that persisted (and which, with official approval, persists).

○ Statistics mean something.

They don't mean much. They are merely tidy footnotes to messy experience. As Frank Lloyd Wright said, 'The truth is more important than the facts.' We have to go beyond the numbers game.

LIST 92   And porky pies

○ Sats results, and the like, measure achievement.

They don't. They measure only what they measure. Can a Sat measure attitude to learning? As Tyrrell Burgess has written, league tables are an 'attempt, so far unsuccessful, to introduce the ethics of football into education' (*The Devil's Dictionary of Education*).

○ Religious schools extend achievement.

They don't. Or if they do, they extend achievement for a minority, usually a middle-class one. And then only measurable improvement.

○ Children come to school to work, not play.

The power of play to aid learning has become neglected. Children should play in the normally accepted usage in KS1, but higher up the school, they should learn, for example about words, by playing with them, and about numbers by playing with them, as in Lists 51–3.

○ Education is primarily a matter of teaching skills and inculcating facts.

No, again. It is, as Margaret Donaldson wrote, about putting children in a situation where they learn in meaningful contexts through trial and error. I would add that it is about helping children to understand new knowledge in terms of the knowledge they already have. The word 'skills' debases real learning, especially in the ghastly phrase 'thinking skills'.

Educational clichés

I have already written that some clichés are clichés because they are true. But there is another kind of cliché that isn't true. It's just sloppy thinking.

Hear these on a course, and listen to the rest dubiously. Or if you can, without getting into trouble, go home.

- ○ Rolling out
- ○ Learning curve
- ○ I can see where you're coming from (unspoken: 'but I think you're an idiot')
- ○ I know what you're saying (see above)
- ○ Best practice (what I think you should do, and the headteacher/ inspector says so anyway, so do it, damn your eyes)
- ○ Mission statement

This is always composed of clichés and platitudes; it is a statement of the obvious. Its real aim is to protect the back of the headteacher and governors. 'In this school we aim at excellence and diversity through a range of pedagogical methods that are accessible to all ethnic groups, and open to both sexes, and all sexual orientations …' Might as well say, we approve of sunlight, apples and children singing. Who wouldn't?

If you can't imagine the opposite of a statement like this, the statement is meaningless. Try it:

> In this school we aim at poor education and use a limited range of methods that are closed to some ethnic groups, and also to women and gays …

- ○ Can we take this on board? (means: 'you'd better')

More clichés

○ Cascading (means 'she's been on a course, and she'd better tell the rest of you about it, and then you can pass it on downwards')

This suggests a model of knowledge, in which the knowledge, or information, doesn't change when it is passed on. In fact, all true learning transforms the learner, the teacher and the knowledge, or information. And, in that process, the learner transforms the learning. On the other hand, according to the deliverers of cascade learning – and that mixed metaphor (how can you deliver a cascade?) speaks volumes – what will be passed on at the bottom of that cascade (lovely word for a crappy thing) will be the same (it is hoped) as what was passed on at the top.

○ Challenging children. And, come to that, challenging parents

These are examples of a special kind of cliché, weasel words: cowardly ones that betray an aversion to telling the truth as the speaker sees it.

○ Appropriate/inappropriate

More weasel words. The speaker means right/wrong, but is afraid to say so.

The Wider Picture 6

LIST 95   Novels relevant to education

○ *The Harpole Report*, by J.L. Carr

Dated, of course; it was published in 1972. I was around at the time, and read the book when it came out, and it seemed to be dated then, rooted in the 1950s. But it is the funniest and most truthful novel about primary education that I know. An innocent young head deals with a staffroom of cynics, hacks and deadbeats, and one wild idealist. One deadbeat says to the head 'I have never been spoken to like that in all my thirty years' experience', and he replies, 'You have not had thirty years' experience. You have had one year's experience thirty times.'

○ *To Sir With Love* by E.R. Braithwaite

Unsentimental story of a Guyanese teacher in a rough London school. 'I love them, these brutal, disarming bastards, I love them . . .'

○ *Hard Times* by Charles Dickens
○ and *David Copperfield*
○ *Jane Eyre* by Charlotte Bronte

See my book *How to teach with a Hangover* (Continuum) for more on these.

Plays

○ *Forty Years On* and *The History Boys* by Alan Bennett

The first deals with a public school putting on a play; the second with comprehensive schoolboys preparing for Oxbridge examinations. Bennett is a genius, and there are great jokes. And lines, some funny, some not, that will burn themselves onto your brain at a second reading/hearing.

○ *Prin* by Andrew Davies

The principal of the title is being bullied out of her job, but as she goes she makes some memorable statements about education.

LIST 97   Memoirs

○ *A Nest of Teachers* by Edward Blishen

This is a terrific account of an ex-servicemen undergoing emergency training after the Second World War. But it has much to say for all teachers.

○ *Molesworth* by Geoffrey Willans and Ronald Searle

Originating in 1953 with the first volume, this very funny book, with perfectly matching drawings by Ronald Searle, has more truth to tell about schools than you might expect. I have read the section called 'Masters at a glance' over a hundred times, I should think, since I was fourteen years old, and I still laugh out loud at an effete, curly-haired man saying 'You may think I'm soft, but I'm hard, damned hard', or the skinny, moustached figure with his body in his gown and his right leg in a mantrap saying 'A joke's a joke chaps but don't go too far'.

○ *Teacher* by Sylvia Ashton-Warner

As Herbert Read wrote, 'Miss Ashton-Warner believes that she has discovered a method of teaching that can make the human being naturally and spontaneously peaceable.'

○ *Brave New School* by Joan Goodman

Shows what our grown-up world looks like to children.

○ *Troublesome Boy* by Harold Rosen

A lovely anthology of writings by one of the best educational minds – at least in the teaching of language.

Film and radio

○ *Dead Poets Society*

Robin Williams plays a progressive teacher in a hidebound private school in the US. The film raises issues about what education is for. When the Williams character says he believes that we should teach boys to think for themselves, the headmaster says 'At this age?' The boys are fifteen.

○ *King Street Junior*

This is a radio series, broadcast intermittently on BBC Radio 4. It is always up to date with the issues it airs, and is brilliant on staffroom relationships. It's worth listening to for the closing credits, over which a hall of children sing 'Farmer, farmer, sow your seed'.

Poems

○ Two poems by D.H. Lawrence

'The Best of School' and 'Last Lesson of the Afternoon' in *The Works of D.H. Lawrence* (Wordsworth Poetry Library).

○ Two poems by Seamus Heaney

'The Play Way'
in *Death of a Naturalist* (Faber).

'Alphabets'
in *The Haw Lantern* (Faber).

○ Two poems by Charles Causley

'School at Four o'Clock' and 'Conducting a Children's Choir' in *Collected Poems* (Macmillan).

○ 'Children's Song' by R.S. Thomas in *Collected Poems* (Macmillan).

○ 'Rising Five' by Norman Nicholson in *Modern Poetry*, ed. John Rowe Townsend (OUP).

○ The second section in 'The Manila Manifesto' beginning 'What you need for poetry ...' from *Out of Danger* by James Fenton (Penguin).

LIST 100

Books that changed my teaching

The Lore and Language of Schoolchildren
The Singing Game
both by Iona and Peter Opie (OUP)
These are lovely, timeless books about childhood. Scholarly, humane, accessible.

Assessing Children's Learning by Mary Jane Drummond (David Fulton)
People talk about child-centred. This really is, and learning-centred.

An Introduction to Curriculum Design and Development by Lawrence Stenhouse (Heinemann)
Behind this starchy title is one of the best books about teaching.

The Education of the Poetic Spirit by Marjorie L. Hourd (Heinemann)
This venerable book (1949) is a beautiful celebration of the place of imagination in education.

The Meaning Makers: Children learning language and using language to learn by Gordon Wells (Hodder & Stoughton)

Young Children Learning by Barbara Tizard and Martin Hughes (Fontana)
These two books changed my sloppy habits of thinking about young schoolchildren, especially working-class schoolchildren, and their language.

The Penguin Book of Childhood, ed. Michael Rosen (Viking)
A depressing but necessary record of adulthood's inhumanity to children from 2000 BC to the present day.

Quotations about education

○ 'Education makes a people easy to lead, but difficult to drive; easy to govern, but difficult to enslave.'

Lord Brougham attr.

○ 'We shall never learn to feel and respect our real calling and destiny, unless we have taught ourselves to consider every thing as moonshine, compared with the education of the heart.'

Walter Scott, Letter

○ 'I am certain of nothing but the holiness of the heart's affections and the truth of the imagination.'

John Keats, Letter

○ 'Fortunately in England, at any rate, education produces no effect whatsoever. If it did, it would prove a serious danger to the upper classes, and probably lead to acts of violence in Grosvenor Square.'

Lady Bracknell in *The Importance of Being Earnest*
by Oscar Wilde

The most intense education is always, ultimately, subversive!

○ 'Life isn't all beer and skittles; but beer and skittles ... must form a good part of every Englishman's education.'

Thomas Hughes, *Tom Brown's Schooldays*

○ 'Teaching is a neurosis.'

A.S. Neill, quoted by Joan Goodman (see List 97)

○ A child said *What is the grass?* Fetching it to me with
   full hands;
   How could I answer the child? I do not know what it is
   any more than he.

Walt Whitman, 'Song of myself'

○ 'I have come that they might have life and have it more abundantly.'

Jesus: St John 10:10